MY NAME IS BEAR

An Auto-bear-ography

NAHKO

www.Nahko.com

Management:
Activist Artists Management
Bernie Cahill & Matt Maher
manager@nahko.com

Booking
(excluding EU + UK):
Partisan Arts
Tom Chauncey
Tom@PartisanArts.com

ISBN: 978-1-5323-5898-2

Design/Production:
CreativeBeans.com/Dante Orazzi

Stories and Lyrics:
All photos by Nahko

MY NAME IS BEAR
is

✔ Printed in the USA

✔ Printed with environmentally-friendly Ink

✔ Printed on elemental chlorine-free (ECF),
sustainably-harvested, stock with recycled content.

For the road: the lover, the moment, the way

Table of Contents

Table of Contents

Foreward

In order to move forward, sometimes we must go back to where it all began. Perhaps, dear reader, you will find a few gems of philosophy among the canvas here. There is music in literature, there is poetry in melody. There is power in our narrative and healing in how we deliver it.

My hope is that you, too, consider your journey to self discovery and return to that fruitful becoming of age where the awakening happens continuously in the limitless moment. There can be peace in tone, design, and form. There can be hope in remembering where we have come from.

In love, Aloha, and playful mischief,

Nahko

— 1 —

DRAGONFLY
Resist and Survive

In Alaska that year, I was 18. Just barely.

Those were the days of wine and mushrooms. Those were the nights the sun never went down. Those were the hours spent down on the river, on that little island; singing, drinking, and studying nature like we were learning a foreign language.

It was on that island one night, during our usual fiestas, when I met the Leo that would shift my direction and usher me into a new chapter of discovery and adventure. It was her story that lured me in. She mirrored my birth mother's story in some wildly definitive ways. At that time, the idea to search for my mother hadn't even crossed my mind. But, this young woman's mirror, I couldn't shake it. Only 14 years old, an Aquarian baby boy, given up for adoption to a lovely Christian family. Our chapter together would be filled with youthful rage, laughter, and an insatiable desire for escape.

When the season ended, I flew back to Portland, hopped in a friends car and ventured down the 101. There was an open invitation from her and her friends to visit and stay at their home in Homer, LA. I had about 20 g's stacked from a lucrative summer, a heartstring plucked by my first POC, and a head full of acid, mushrooms, cocaine or whatever else I could get my hands on.

I was transforming. And writing about it. The old archetype was dying, and the new was bursting at the seams. I wanted to feel it all but be responsible for nothing. I started living with no limit, in search of my edge.

I stayed in that little house with too many people for too few beds. I remember the dry ground. Listening for tornados. Regis and Kathy Lee. Risk. Lucy, the pup I found at a Walmart parking lot in Dallas and

brought with me. The house we'd get our yay from. I remember our little family. The people that would look at me in bewilderment, like where are you from boy? The people that would look at her and me together and shake their heads. We were outcasts, both in our own ways. We were hippies becoming.

It was an interim period. A dog-eared page that I often go back to and wonder what it was all about. I learned about resistance in that house. I survived that which could have yielded heavier consequences. We nearly had a child. But, the ghosts live on. Finding the courage to seek and confront myself becoming was the single greatest gift I received on the wings of that psychedelic dragonfly.

*"I started living with no limit
in search of my edge."*

— 2 —

DRAGONFLY

You should put that cigarette out.
You should have faith in my mouth.
Like my mother, like your son,
Like my temperamental lungs
Each piece fits into the next
Like I'm not black and I'm not white.
Both revere me in my sight

You've got twinkles in your eyes
You say, "vegetarians save lives"
But there's your wings despite my back
There's your baby's bassinet
Will there be one more of me?
Close my eyes and try to hide
From my former Dragonfly

Little Bear woke in the woods
Chipped and pealed vehicle hoods
In that van under the covers
I've been stealing from my lover

DRAGONFLY

Moments I cannot replace
To my former Dragonfly
I resist and I survive

What a state I've brought this to
Logic lies of mine pull through
But what's that say of my character?
I retreat back into nature.
Will there be one more of me?
To my form of Dragonfly
I resist and I survive

I will survive.   I will survive.
I will survive.

This is resistance.

— 3 —

SING HIM OF MY REVELATIONS
North, to Alaska

I was 19 that year, driving from Portland to Alaska. I'd spent the first half of winter holed up in a little town in northwestern Louisiana. There was more of us in that house than there were beds. We were fresh from our first summer working seasonal jobs and for me, fresh from leaving the confines of my parent's home for good. Everything was new, limitless, and a little scary. I didn't last longer than two or three months down there in the Arklatex. I'd spent most my money on the road trip to get there. A little chunk went to that blue Dodge caravan I'd bought in Crescent City. The seller, Sleepy's 'friend,' put that first hit of LSD in my gut and opium in my lungs. I'd already decided to buy the van when my heights got higher. The moon was full of course, and there was no stopping the portal opening that night. Anyhow, back to the cash. My bills kept getting traded for too much cocaine cut with god knows what from who knows where. I liked the clammy hands and the fear of dying back then. My sense of self was nonexistent other than I knew I wanted to find my edge and tease the line. I thank my spirit guides for never letting me shoot anything up back then. I wasn't in that bad of a way. I tried little bits of everything though. It's a wonder I didn't dive in with no restraints considering where I'd come from and my abrupt introduction to the world of sex, drugs, and rock 'n roll. It's a wonder I had any self-control at all.

By the time I left that little parish, I was down to my last few bills. I said goodbye to the tornado air and my fistful of friends and caught a Greyhound back to Portland. I found a job washing dishes at an Italian gourmet pizza joint. I camped out in my van for the remainder of winter, waiting for April and spring so that I could drive back to Alaska. Come to find out; they wouldn't hire me back as the swaggering rag time piano player/music director at the dinner theater. Likely I was swaggering too much for their liking. I wasn't the best they'd ever had. I mean c'mon, I was 18, fresh off the boat, and definitely showed up to work tripping, high, drunk, or a mixture of all of those. Life was an adventure, and I was just trying to get amongst it. I couldn't have cared less about a bunch of rich, white tourists who wanted me to play their favorite '40s tunes at the snap of a finger.

I could fake it enough for their liking and tips. I quickly learned how to play them and it, of course, was much easier once I'd convinced them to order more drinks from the bar. Last call now. Liquor makes the show go quicker. That, of course, was one of the tunes I'd play.

Anyhow, back to washing dishes and living in my van. The curve was a hard one to learn. Where to shower. Where to shit. Where to park at night.

Once I learned they weren't going to hire me back on the floor at the dinner theater; I applied for a cooking position in the kitchen there instead. I wasn't going to pass up another opportunity to spend my summer there. I didn't know what else to do with myself except go back to that place and make more memories.

At this stage, I'd convinced my brother Joshua to join me. He and I were quite different, but shared a similar sense of necessity for adventure and living on some kind of edge.

Damn. We packed that van full of everything imaginable for camping and summer fun. Two mountain bikes, a BMX, camping gear, a kayak, skateboards, and who knows what else. Sleepy Brian joined us en route to the Canadian border and so began the caravan to Alaska. I think Bright Eye's record 'I'm Wide Awake It's Morning' had just dropped, so naturally, it became our anthem. It was SO our life. 'So we're parking in ally, just hoping that our shit is safe.' Definitely our story. Cheers-ing Molson on the Alkan Highway under April stars, glinting with Borealis mist. Just enough cash to get to our summer jobs, just enough fucks given to make a pathway to something tangible. Sleepy had driven this route before so he had a few pit stops up his sleeve that definitely gave fever to the still winter crawl. It was early April with snow still on the land, but warm enough to be melting it off the roads. Slush brown burms layered the highways as we drove north, with the heat broken in my van and blankets covering our frozen bodies.

Liard hot springs. If you ever get the chance, go there. It might be the first hot springs this Bear ever touched. The scene is too good to forget though. Steam rising from the waters after a long walk down a wooden pathway. La luna rose to greet our youthful wonder, and my body began to tingle with the waters healing massage. And then as if to peek us into another dimensional trip, the sky began to wisp and swirl. I nearly spit out my beer. There she was. In all her glory. Miss Aurora Borealis. Damn, she fine. My eyes could barely hold back the water. It was surreal. Like I was in a movie I grew up fantasizing about. As if there were beings giving us a light show before they took us back to Taurus. So, I took another sip of my Molson. Got neck deep in that sulfuric mineral bath and gave into my mystical imagination. What a world is this!

By the time we crossed the Yukon border, my brother and I were properly frozen in our seats. If I'd had a moustache at the time, it would undoubtedly have had icicles on it. We parked at a turnout that night, facing out to Lake Teslin. As per usual, we awoke to frost and my own breath crystalizing in front of me. This morning was different though. This morning the fuel line would explode. Soon as I turned the key, gas began spraying everywhere. My heart sank.

It took what seemed hours for a AAA rep to find someone in Teslin to come up to the turnout and take a look at the damage. This classic, callused old native fella in his overalls pulled up in a four-door Camry a cigarette hanging out his mouth. It was a cold morning. He took a few looks, made a few calls on his flip phone, and turned back to me shaking his head. It would take days to get the part in, and it would cost me more than I had in my pocket, and that was all

I had to get to my job. I had no choice but to ditch
the van. So, we dumped some clothes and a bike into
Sleepy's Volvo and waved goodbye. Posting up on the
side of the highway in the snow, we waited. The look
on my brother's face was priceless. I'd been through
some helpless moments before, but this was a whole new
level of excitement, dread, and a test of our youthful perseverance. We managed to hitchhike nearly a
thousand miles to Denali in three days. We slept on
park benches and bus stations, which were basically
someone's front yard. By the time we reached Denali,
we were a piece of work. I think my brother had had
enough of my style of traveling. He disappeared into
the abyss of the resort. We worked different shifts
and areas of the resort and didn't see much of each
other that summer. It wasn't long after we got there
that we got the news from home; dad had been diagnosed

with cancer. That same summer, my sister went through
multiple miscarriages as she tried to birth her first
child. My brother was less fortunate than I with his
hand at drugs and I remember my parents pleading me to
look after him, for fear he would not return. My way
at that time with him was my own type of tough love.

Show him the way to freedom, but he had to carve his own path from there. He had wanted out, and I gave him the ride, but I couldn't be responsible for him after that. I felt guilty for years. He eventually came around and got his life together. It was a hard year for all of us until then.

"I had no teachers, I sought no text. I wanted to see it with my own eyes. To believe it. To touch it."

My father went through some pretty serious treatment after that summer. We weren't sure if he would make it past winter, but he ended up living for another five years. At the time I wrote this song, I had yet to make peace with the man I called dad. There would be many years to follow where I tried to come to terms with him and his ways, my birth father, and his ways. Looking back, I never respected my dad the way a boy should. There was a window as a child where I did look up to him. But it was short lived. It took the years leading up to his passing for me to understand him, let go of my reckless anger. To find peace in who he was and adoration for what he stood for.

I can still hear the angst in the last verse of this song, as I take an outside perspective in the storytelling to say 'Laying in his cell confined to just euphoric, painless memories in mind. The nurse can't seem to tell if he's alright there's silence from his wife. IV sense him dreaming of his children, does he really even know them? There's no pain, but this cancer can't be good, so I am hanging on his every word, pleading you've done the best you could.' You can sense me softening a bit even there. I wanted him to see the world as I was beginning to see it. I wanted him to know why I was so angry, yet the resolve to that anger came at a later time, in a song that had yet to be written.

My reconciling with Creator is so evident here as I didn't yet know what to call that which gave life to all things. To me, the cycle of life was dark and horrible, but in the same breath, I sought the magic of nature to calm my ferocious appetite for understanding. So, I called the Creator a beast. Humans, nature, religion. It was all too complex for me at that time. I had no teachers; I sought no text. I wanted to see it with my own eyes. To believe it. To touch it. To bleed for and with it. There was no other way. And, I got what I wanted. Through sacrifice I found connection. Through ceremony I found purpose. This story, however, is far from over. I've always wanted to say it, so here it is my dear reader; to be continued.

— 4 —

SING HIM OF MY REVELATIONS

Hello rainbow. What an afternoon
you've chosen to appear to us.

You're looking quite, quite lovely.
How are my friends those clouds?

Sweet, sweet mother don't you cry again.
My sister spoke of children dying,
dying in her womb.

Brother, keep your wallet underneath
the covers. When the snow comes.

Winter gets so cold, so cold my palms
can sweat no more.

So I reach for my head and I
understand nothing.

I reach for a constellation that seems to be
growing, growing stronger than me.

Built by a beast.

Blue van. Driving north thru Canada. So
long, oh Louisiana and a fist full a friends.

Yukon. Nothing here but emptiness though
somehow I feel the most comforted

With no one. With no heat and no telling
where we'll wake up next.

Liard springs to life the warmest waters.
Cleansing. And oh my god what's the matter
with the sky?

Look! Look! Here it comes that Borealis!
Mine eyes have not seen anything like it!

What a world is this!

So I reach for my head and I
understand nothing.

I reach for a constellation that seems to be
growing, growing stronger than me.

Built by a beast.

Laying in his cell confined to just euphoric,
painless memories in mind

The nurse can't seem to tell if he's alright.
There's silence from his wife.

IV sends him dreaming of us children.
Does he really even know them?

There's no pain, but this cancer can't be
good so I am hanging on his every word

Pleading you've done the best you could.

His face weak from all the medication I'm
determined to sing him of my revelations

Send him on his way.

Well, pa I'm sure you are in line with
whatever you've got coming.

But, I'm sure there were times you felt
absolutely nothing

At all in your head

At all in your bed

— 5 —

KIRBY, JOE
That One Time I Ate Rocks

Three different mushroom trips with three different people at three different places and times. True
story.

1: A gorgeous summer day in Alaska. Kirby and I
were hauling ass down dirt trails on our bicycles,
flying high on magic mushrooms. I could hear the bugs
whizzing around us. Even the trees seemed to laugh
with us as we cackled at the afternoon freedom from
our summer jobs. We were happy. We were high. Every adventure we went on in that national park was a
chance to discover something new; about the park and
yourself. This trip was no different.

We found ourselves down a side trail, sliding on
rocks and bunny hopping tree roots, down to where it
ended at a creek. Or maybe it was a river? It doesn't
matter. What did matter was the grandfather tree that
watched over it. Kirby was immediately in the water,
gasping at the colorful rocks and shimmering water. I
saw the old tree, and it's banana swoop trunk and mon-
keyed up it in a heartbeat. There I was, standing on
this long branch as it hung over the river, grasping
its limbs with my own. I must have gotten carried away
with being all at one with the tree in that shuffle
because before I knew it, I fell out of the ancient
one's embrace and landed hard on the ground. I must
have forgotten gravity was a thing because I thought
there was no need to hang on anymore. Metaphors for

life, I suppose. Kirby and I bellowed with laughter at the fall. In no time I walked into the middle of the river where Kirby was collecting rocks and climbed atop a large boulder protruding from the waters. I began to hum. Again.

I had been humming this tune since we began our journey. It was something like a polka. Every time I would hum it, I laughed. I could hear the tuba. I could hear the French horn. It was hilarious.

So, it kept coming out of me, that tune. And as I stood there, gazing down at Kirby showing me little rocks that sparkled in the midday sun, I wondered what it would be like to eat one. They just looked so deli-cious. I can't remember whose idea it was to eat one, but it seemed completely rational at the time. As I write this, I can still taste the rock's minerals in my mouth, and the purity of that glacier water as it hit my tongue and fell into my stomach. Gulp.

"Recklessness was much better shared with a lover, under the radar, and under the influence."

And still, I gazed down at my friend in the river and thought of perspective. From his spot, every-thing appeared a certain way. From my vantage point, another. I believe it was then I began to see more clearly how people are. It was then I began to under-stand grace.

2: It must have been the winter that followed when I found myself sitting across the table from my youth-ful reflection in love and mischief. There's a place on Belmont in SE Portland that invites you to smoke hooka, eat cheese and fruit, and drink wine. There's

nothing better to digest magic mushrooms with than
these, I reckon. It was only a matter of minutes before our bodies began to tingle and we wanted nothing
more than to soak in that Cascadian air. To feel the
pulse of the night. We ran into the park. We were
kids again. And, well, we were kids. There was a
sense of adventure, everything was new, and cartwheels
got the blood rushing and the laughter bellowing. We
knew it would end. Or perhaps it would turn into something even more magical.   There were tastes, smells,
and colours that would stay for weeks after. I suppose the medicine broke down our walls and guided us

through the night on an epic field trip to the heart
of nature, symbiosis, and intimacy. Just pieces of a
narrative we experienced in our becoming of age.

3: October 6th, 2006. After having spent my second
summer pillaging the central valley in Denali, I left
Alaska and headed to the piko of the Pacific. Tick-
ets were cheap, and there was a work trade program I
got turned onto that I was excited about: W.W.O.O.F.
Willing Workers on Organic Farms. I'd checked it out
and booked myself a few farms to work at. I was get-

ting used to traveling alone and finding my way around. Used to not having money or tools to get by except my songs and presence.

So there I was, in my REI shorts, long bushy Alaskan beard, lip ring, and huge traveler's backpack. I'd met Jason within the first couple days on island. I was staying at the Hilo Hostel, and before I hitched to my first farm job in South Kona, I stopped by his work trade in Papaikou. Jason picked me up at the bottom of his huge, steep hill - dirt all over him, cigarette hanging from his grinning mouth, and a 12 pack of Sierra Nevadas on the back of his little scooter. I hopped on with my 2 million pound backpack, and we started up the hill. We looked like Dumb and Dumber with all our shit, especially me with that backpack and 12 pack hanging off the end of a scooter barely big enough for Jason as it was. But, we were about to have the most legendary conversation of our lives. Well, at least of mine at the time. For some reason, he was asking me about my family, and for some reason, I was already on what my birth/adopted names are. When I got to the part about my native name, the one given to me by my grandmother, he was like, ' Wait, that's your middle name? Nacho cheese or whatever? Why don't you go by that?' We then had a short discussion on the practicality of it. It just seemed too long. No one would get it. Well, you could cut it in half, and it would just be … Nahko. I chuckled, turned my head around to see the panoramic ocean view and whispered it to the horizon. Nahko. What a weird and wild ride I was on. No better time to start fresh. We pulled up to the farm, and Jason's host greeted us. He shook my hand and smiled. 'Aloha, I'm River. Welcome.' I shrugged off my backpack, cracked open a beer, sighed deeply and replied, 'Mahalo. My name is Nahko.'

— 6 —

KIRBY JOE

We were tripping out to this riff
in our heads

Something that goes like this
but comes out way different

Kinda like your first kiss.

In those times just in time I fell out of
some trees

Low I lay and saw the world so clearly

And in all the right colors.

In the sky. In the sky. In the sky.

In the sky to the ground.
From the waters to your mouth.

I can see it from this river bed of ours.

One hooka, some cheese, ma'am check please!

Out into the streets we ran so childishly...
cuz why does it matter?

Two young lovers with room to grow

Let's see who can do three cartwheels
in a row

Cuz why does it matter?

Don't ask why. Don't ask why.
Don't ask why.

Don't ask why. I won't lie.
They were two kids getting high.

Off of life and their love for each other.

Our faces glowed from our epiphanies

As we ate like kings from banana trees

And felt relieved to be going swimming.

The Milky Way's got a way with me

Am I really here? Or am I just dreaming on
my way out to sea?

We will sail. We will sail. We will sail.

We will sail off the earth.

And find out just how it works.

To believe in something that embodies matter.

If you see what I see from where I'm standing

What you've shown me can only get better.

— 7 —

BE HERE NOW
And Be Here Later

It was November 2006. Hot as shit outside. They called this place Captain Cook. I'd read the stories of that guy. How he'd 'discovered' a lot of places this side of the seven seas. His facade as a god ran out on the Big Island. Just down the road from where I was working is where he was slaughtered in the sand. In the looming shadows of the Kealakekua Bay cliffs, where they would bury their royalty.

When I signed up for Willing Workers on Organic Farms [WWOOF], there wasn't a bone in my body that knew hard labor. Yet, my subconscious knew I would over-come the rough start, and my blood knew that my future ancestor would awaken and get my hands dirty, as my people have always done.

I spent nearly three months in South Kona. Writing songs, picking coffee, harvesting lettuce, grooming trees, building things. I had two gurus at my first work trade. They seemed like total opposites in doc-trine, but naturally similar in essence. Andy was a profoundly angelic creature. A marvelously talented cellist, a man of the lord, a real island monkey. He was the first to call me Nahkohe-ese. Hemonsu was the quiet, hard-working coffee plantation owner with pro-found wisdom in the little he said. He and his wife both had adopted Hindi names, which intrigued me and helped me settle into my own reclaimed name.

I found Ram Dass's book "Be Here Now" in the library at that farm. Or was it in a box somewhere? I can't seem to remember exactly. It found me. But, when it did it was exactly when I needed it. It quickly became my scripture. Each page cradled my longing for a teaching that could ease me through the transformation I was experiencing. That old archetype was dying. It wasn't long before I was able to begin applying the poetic mantras to my daily life.

Of course, there's always some kind of muse whence the song came to me. There was a girl, naturally. Thank god. She was a catalyst in the lessons of youthful, reckless love and the struggle of intimacy with-

out expectation of commitment. Be here now. Enjoy the ride. Don't tell anyone how to live their life, but know how you will live yours - with boundaries, but on an open road to courageous self-security.

The story in this song is a real thing. It happened. When I listen to it now, I grin. Always trust the symphony in your head. Love without limit, but when you find your edge - respect it.

I can still see that yellow school bus, the lettuce and basil, and that twinkle in my higher reflection as if to say 'It's a long road ahead, kid. Be present and kind. Only good things can come of it.'

"Don't tell anyone how to live their life, but know how you will live yours - with boundaries, but on an open road to courageous self-security. "

— 8 —

BE HERE NOW

You've got two feet that seem to keep
wandering away from me

Your curiosity is kind of irritating and by
that I mean you're not alone

I was waiting on you.
You were waiting on me. So in silence we'd
sit wondering, wondering.

From your mind down your shoulders to your
right hand

Onto paper into history you're making plans.

You've lost your wonder for me, but not for
the land.

Be here now. Be here now. While you are
still around. I'm gonna be here now.

He will enchant you take you
under a waterfall and kiss you.

There will be no sleeping cuz he's brand new
and you dreamed this too.

And then your mind slips to who you're
supposedly with

And you say oh shit but his grip is tingling
your fingertips so why bother with it

And he's saying to you

Be here now. Come on baby, just be here now.
While I am still around. Be here now.

Be here now. Be here now. While I am still
around. Just, be here now.

By mellow candlelight we write in our old
school bus

Too tired of arguing so we've just given up

And in the background I hear enough is enough

So I started moving further west

Just me and my machine and what we manifest

We are well worn we are blessed

I see a city fuel my fight - I see some damn
good years in the countryside

I see a quite quite life

There's a tall brick building in the middle
of town

That's where several years later she still
lives by the vow

The same words to this day I like to sing out
loud

I'm gonna be here now. Be here now. While
we are still around. Be here now.

— 9 —

GOODNIGHT, SUN
This Little Light of Mine

This is my salutation. A sun song. Kealakekua Bay
is an old place. There's a viewpoint as you come down
the highway that I remember sitting on after work and
basking in the most epic sunsets. Those vistas, they
were like paintings. All sun, a little sky, and an
equally infinite ocean. I would perch there on certain days when it felt right. It was all about fear-
lessness then. Doing things I didn't know how to do so
I could get over being scared to try it. I was pretty
skinny back then. Huge beard on my face, lip ring,
long hair down to my butt. I lived at a couple of different farms over my time there. To tell you the truth
I can't remember exactly which one I was at when this
song was birthed. What I remember is the turn out off
the highway where I sat and watched the sunset. There
it was, all fiery and red and taking up the whole sky.
And there I was, high on mushrooms or LSD, singing to
it as it set fell into the ocean. What a wondrous
thing it was to witness. There's a familiar newness
and innocence of those precious awakening moments.

There is poetry in this love song to Ra. A tinge of
loneliness can be felt in the words 'Am I as prideful
as you say that I am? I mumble loudly and work thru
the silence'. Fumbling and awkward are great ways to
describe how my social skills were back then. Well,
I'll give myself a little more credit in saying that by
the time I'd been in Hawaii for a few months my ability
to interact with humans had gotten loads better. Even

with two summers in Alaska and a winter in Louisiana, my ability to be outgoing had overcome the much lower level of anxiety or insecurity that I'd left home with. So, despite depression teasing my every step to self-love, 'this little light of mine will brighten up a dark place' is exactly what I focused on.

Without the sun's positive vibration shining down on me each day, I don't know if I would have learned such skills to survive. I spent a lot of time outdoors and in the ocean because of it. Learned to sweat, bleed, and enjoy being in and of the earth. The sun would never complain or take me for granted. I was always at her mercy. And she would charge me up just enough for the moon to take over and continue my wonderment with life, creation, and love songs. And so it was. My salvation was solar, and my heart beamed with circles around the moon.

— 10 —

GOODNIGHT, SUN

Goodnight sun. I love the colors you've
chosen to close with.

Goodnight sun.
And the rays and how they are woven.

Watching me watch you fall over the ocean.

Putting a spin on my inner emotion.

Warming my face to this evening's devotion.

I hope someone else sees you how
I see you seeing me.

Do you recall what we spoke of last evening?

You said that I need to be more forgiving.

I was ashamed that you caught me believing

I could fix all of my problems by leaving.

Off in the distance I heard someone singing

Goodnight sun!   Goodnight sun!

Goodnight sun.
Did you see me stretch and wave good morning?

Goodnight sun.
And I love the way you look in the morning

28

GOODNIGHT, SUN

Am I as prideful as you say that I am?

I mumbly loudly and work thru the silence

The only thing constant is your
humble presence

To the other side of the world get ready
for the message of the sun of the sun!

Goodnight sun. You're amber orange
and autumn. Goodnight sun.

I won't be one who's forgotten your glory.

If I awake and I cannot see your face.

This little light of mine will brighten up
a dark place.

I can see clearly now what I am to do

All of the changes and struggles
I tremble thru with you.

Goodnight sun!   Goodnight sun!

Good evening moon.

This is my salutation. You are my salvation.

— 11 —

ALICE
When the Giants Come

The warm, light winds of South Kona would typically wake me from my slumber on the lanai in those days. Coqui would chirp me to sleep under the watchful eye of my star relative, Ursa Minor. I was working quite a lot at that time. I baked at a banana bread shop, was a clerk at the natural food store, landscaped, hustled ganja. On the side, I would moonlight at whatever local jam there was to share my songs. A couple of my friends from Alaska had moved there, and I was renting their back porch as my abode. There was enough space for a small mat, guitar case, and a hikers backpack. It was all I needed. One morning, however, on that peaceful lanai I was abruptly awoken from a dream. Heart racing, sweat dripping from my brow, and tears pouring from my eyes, I vividly remembered what I had seen in that lucid state. It was my first waking dream that I can recall. Up until then remembering dreams when woken consisted of mainly being chased by bad guys or catastrophic events and escaping nature's deadly path. Quite frankly, I die a lot in my dreams. This particular dream wasn't scary, necessarily, but definitely revealing and confrontational.

It began with a chase through the coffee fields, a place I had been spending plenty of my time in picking and planting. My prey was a friend of mine whom I'd had no beef with in real life, but in my dreams, we were volleying for a woman and apparently he had stepped onto my proclaimed turf. So a chase was in

order. When I finally caught up to him, we battled
with ... rocks? He managed to slam his into my hands,
and in a moment of terror, my hands turned black. I
held up my black hands in horror, and the entire scene
shifted. Then I was walking quickly through a crowded
street. The tall skyscrapers reminded me of New York,
and as I passed two police officers, I tucked my head
and ducked into a bustling mall. This scene will always conjure a 'Where's Waldo' page. So many people,
where's Bear? Weaving between the suits and dresses,

I walked right into a very long table in the middle
of the mall with a man and woman sitting at it. They
were dressed in suits and seemed to have been waiting
for me. There's a chair in front of them, and they
gestured for me to take a seat. This was my judgement
day. Sorrow came over me as I realized I was here
to be reckoned with. My black hands were put on the
table, cuffed by a guard, and just then I saw two men
walking by smirking. I screamed, ' You'll get yours!'
in anger and sadness. The woman tsk'ed and shook her
head. 'So much anger...a shame.' The man promptly
took over and asked me ' Do you know why you're here?'
It was without question that I knew I was to be pun-

ished for my violent retaliation towards my friend in the coffee field. I could barely raise my head and replied, 'I've done a lot of bad things in my life.' As the tears began to well, a man out of nowhere appeared from the crowd. He bore no recognizable face, just wearing a brown trench coat and a briefcase in his left hand. He walked directly up to me, I stood up with a little surprise and quickly walked into his arms. He held me with such understanding and comfort that the tears welling fell reluctantly. It was in that forgiving embrace that I woke abruptly from my slumber, tears falling from my cheeks, sweat swallowing my sheets.

It's always so fascinating to me what our REM cycle pulls from our daily waking life. I used to hitchhike from my house to my work at the natural food store. Every week, at least once or twice, the same dude would pick me up on his way home from work and give me a

> "A world without doors is not a home.
> A world without the maze is a nightmare.
> A world made of riddles is a dream come true.
> For what do we live for, but solutions and answers."

lift. My stop was on his route. It was there in the passenger seat of his old VW bus that I learned about the giants and the key in which the universe resonates in. The sun would be setting as I took a pull from his pipe and his words would go on and on about the philosophy of time and the prophecy unfolding. Imagine being high as a kite and hearing stories about giants. Giants that created the earth and buried themselves beneath it eons ago. Soon a war would come where we would fight alongside angels and giants as the 12th planet returned to reclaim what man could not hold sacred. I would say 'Far out, man.' and drift off into a resonance of thought and wonder. He'd say things like 'Y'know the universe is in B flat, and its color is deep purple?' I'd say things like 'Ho, bra, no way... mentals.' We would laugh and then it was 'shoots see you next time.' The magnificence in his story about the giants sat deep with me. After all, when I was adopted, I was named after a king in the Bible who fought a giant. I believed in them, not because of that story, but because it only made sense that our bodies had changed with the planet over time. All the superhuman powers could still be accessed with the right teachers, but perhaps they had been lost for centuries. Regardless, I knew not that this was the beginning of my mystical teachings. But, I'm so happy this song still lives because it is a direct connection to the beginning of my work in the multidimensional field of songwriting and dream telling.

I'd gone down the rabbit hole. I begin the song by telling Alice I'm well aware of the strange and complex world she lives in, and I will not be visiting. Not so wonderland, after all, the weird and mystical. However, I am no coward. Courage becomes me as I journey through the maze and tap into my awakening power. Superhuman. Not immortal, yet I survive Alice's puzzle and rise from my slumber with ultimate respect for her design. In closing, I bow. A world without doors is not a home. A world without the maze is a nightmare. A world made of riddles is a dream come true. For what do we live for, but solutions and answers.

— 12 —

ALICE

Alice, Alice I'm well aware. That there are
some strange things where you live.

And I won't go there.

Down which hallway and thru which door.
What's this wonderland here for?

Turn my cards queen of hearts says you will
go there.

Busy, busy busy bees. These humans are such
mysteries. Floating around and never knowing
what they want.

So go forth. Go forth with your morning
dear. With the sun arms on your back and the
love that you left behind.

First of all, it was the year of the boar.
And they greeted you with horns on your passenger door in the middle of traffic on the
morning of our full moon.

Fleeing into the coffee fields, I'm dragging
guilt tied to my heals. My friend, he is
coming, and he means to reckon with me.

Favor his hands blackened by fire. Favor our
tempers and boyish desires. There's a reason

that you came to me lucidly in my sleep.

I am no coward. You're superhuman. Tapped
into power.

The load is heavy. Will you be ready when
the giants come? Well, I will be there.

"You'll get yours!" came out of my mouth. To
the man who bound my hands I began to scream
and I began to shout.

Sir, I know I've done many terrible things
and I'm concerned to find they find me in my
dreams. Such bad behavior I am not the same.

Amid all my rage, disguised as a man, an an-
gel appeared with briefcase in hand. Didn't
speak when he reached he just held me like
you hold someone you love.

Cradled I wept right out of my slumber.
Writing it down this is what I remember.
There's a reason that you came to me lucidly
in my sleep.

I am no coward. You're superhuman. Tapped
into power.

The load is heavy. Will you be ready when
the giants come? Well, I will be there.

I WILL BE THERE. I WILL BE THERE. I WILL BE
THERE. I WILL BE THERE.

ALICE

WHEN THE GIANTS COME!

Alice, Alice I'm well aware. That there are
some strange things where you live and I have
been there.

— 13 —

EARLY FEBRUARY
Where is Your God?

I used to sleep in a 17x11 tent on 6 acres, 2 miles up Captain Cook Road under a canopy of Mac nut trees. I would do a few days of work trade for a place to pitch my tent and cook my ramen. Al owned the little lot and lived across the road. I think he served in Vietnam and bought his land years and years ago. He taught me to sail and picked me up hitchhiking one day and offered the tent space if I could help out with some landscaping and building projects. Scott was in the truck with him that day when he pulled over to give me a ride. Scott was my Steve Mcqueen. He was filled with wild stories of truly living life and escaping the law. I was in awe of him. He loved it when I sang into the trees at night. I loved both him and Al because they were tortured souls like myself, but chose to emanate aloha and live with the soil and salt. Scott and I formed a particularly beautiful bond up there on the hill. We shared a common dream. He dreamt of returning to his two kids back in Atlanta. The law was in his way. I had a budding vision to know my mother. I had to find her in my way.

I didn't know the first thing about finding a miss-ing person. In fact, the thought of looking for my mom hadn't even crossed my mind yet. During my stay up Captain Cook Road, I began to unravel a bit of the wonder and mystery around the whole story with Scott. He'd ask hard to answer questions. I would dig into his story, too. We challenged each other as brothers to go further than before. What was stopping us from fulfilling these visions? Ourselves.

At that time, I'd seen a handful of letters my mom used to write to me. We lost contact with her around the time I was five years old because she moved around a lot. Since the adoption was private, the letters would come through a caseworker. My parents let me read the letters when I was 17. Mom would always sign her letters with a note that usually read something like, " Don't be mad at me. I didn't have a choice. Please find me when you're ready. " And then she would sign it with her social security number. I remember

reading that and thinking 'aww ma why would I ever be mad at you!?' Skip ahead four years or so, there I am smoking a joint with Scott under a blanket of stars chatting about the letters. He was quizzing me on the details of my mom's story and whereabouts. I sighed. I didn't know much. What I did gather was that my birth was not planned and my mom suffered be-cause of it. This truth had barely even begun to rear its weight.

It was pretty ironic to write this song and not two weeks later find my mother. Talk about a quick turn around manifestation! I wrote a pretty basic play by play that depicted in verse one my mama's journey, in verse two my father's part in the madness, and my own tortured moment in verse three. Their story wasn't completely accurate, but it got the point across. How could there be a god? How could he/she/it let this kind of horrible thing to happen? Yes, of course, my life was a product of it, and I was grateful, but at such a cost! "I saw her fall, fall, fall on her knees in sorrowful respect for the child she leaves. Tell me where is your god now." There's a bit of spite in those words, I reckon. Not much, but I can feel a little of the frustration I was carrying in just the not knowing of truth. So, I spilled my heart into a song. I was born in early February. An unexpected gift to the world. This was the beginning of my trials and tribulations. I was taking my first steps onto that galactic highway towards self-discovery and scribbling bits of songs onto jungle worn pieces of paper, strewn about my 17x11. It's a wonder I archived the melodies into my memory bank and weren't lost along the journey. It's a wonder I survived long enough to tell the tale.

— 14 —

EARLY FEBRUARY

There was one born early February.
On an icy afternoon.

She was far too young to even carry.
So they gave her options out.

And she knew she wasn't even ready.

So she used her head and instead put the baby
in the bed of a woman she'd never met

And she let go. So many years ago.
So many years ago.

And she wonders where he roams.
Wonders where he roams.

I saw her fall, fall, fall. Fall on her
knees. In sorrowful respect for the child
who leaves.

Tell me where, tell me where is your god now?

On the dock at 7:30.
Dressed and pressed in white.

Proudly represents his countries navy.
Now it's time to have some fun.

Out on leave he meets a pretty lady.
And created me.

His folks were wealthy, the girl not looking
healthy

So they advised him to run.
Run from his son.
Run from his son his firstborn was mistaken

For a smoking gun.
Father look what you have done.

I saw him fall, fall, fall.

Fall on his knees.
In sorrowful respect for the child who
leaves.

Tell me where, tell me where is your god
now?

In my van I shook with violent treason.
Oh, Columbia Gorge!

Hold my mama's picture as I'm dreaming.
Of my baby sisters who are they?

Got a lot of longing for my kin.
And what of you little brother?

Have you respect for your mother?
And your native tongue?

Oh these lungs breathe * *

In your dreams...little brother where have
you gone?

And so I fall, fall, fall.

Fall on my knees. In sorrowful respect for
the child who leaves.

Tell me where, tell me where is your god
now?

— 15 —

CALL HIM BY HIS NAME
Baby Brothers Baby

I was living on the farm up Hamakua when my brother found out he was going to be a father. He was the first of us kids to have a child. None of us thought he would be the first, only because he, much like me, was floating in a sea of possibilities. Young, rebellious, and unlikely to follow the rules. I knew he would come around and rise up with this child. In fact, I remember feeling excited for him to reverse the perception our parents may have had of him. These verses flow between reflecting on my brother and on my own relationship at the time. I was in love and in a very curious, explorative space. How does a man treat his woman? How do I respect her? Thank the gods that she had the patience to see me through all my stumbling and shortcomings. Through the mistakes of youth, my partner at the time truly loved me 'just the same.' I learned to reflect that same way with my brother. I

> *"Your rivers courses may shift,*
> *but you remain water together."*

wrote this over a period of a year or so. Dim yellow light shining through the window on the face of my beloved. Droplets of rain glistened on the sill. Those Hilo nights were thick with precipitation. Like swimming in a pool of atmospheric pressure. Gentle, but memorable. We used to drive a vegetable oil Mercedes. I can still smell it. Using less, accomplishing more. You can feel the joy in this melody. Such were the times. Life was light. Life was playful.

This was the beginning of my journey to honoring a sacred bond. I would make mistakes along the way. My imperfections were beautiful, but I had yet to see them as such. In many ways, my brother's growth was reflecting a similar journey. We'd drifted apart, but a brothers bond never breaks. The courses of your rivers may shift, but you remain water together.

"This was the beginning of my journey to honoring a sacred bond."

— 16 —

CALL HIM BY HIS NAME

City sleeps, but not my youngest brother.
He's the first of us an unexpected father.

Laying silent lonely apartment.
He swears he'll be a better parent.

Than his mother's loose foundation.
He won't crumble or sink into the ocean.

He's fitting into a grown man's shoes.
Whether or not he was ready or ever wanted
to.

So I call him by his name. I say you're not
to blame. I love you just the same.

I love you just the same.

Yellow light befalls my window.
Casting lines upon your shadow.

What a selfless firm foundation.
I've surpassed past liberation.

Bind us by similar karma.
Hold me to personal dharma.

I will not be taking chances.
Holding fast to brittle branches.

So I call her by her name. I say you're not
to blame. I love you just the same.

CALL HIM BY HIS NAME

I love you just the same.

Oh, for man to see.
How to treat his queen.
To keeping your hands free.
To carry all she needs.

To be what she perceives.
You've made yourself out to be.

And to call her by her name.
To say you're not to blame.
I love you just the same.

I love you just the same.

— 17 —

CREATION'S DAUGHTER
Stoned on a Stone

I literally was stoned on a stone. My road dog, Sleepy Brian, loaded a pipe with ganja salad and hash dressing. There we were in the late summer sunshine, a few Alaskan road trips under our belt and an adventure in front of us. I'd left my four jobs, girlfriend, and community in South Kona to follow the flow again. It had been a good first year on the island, but now it was time to explore. I had a ticket to Burning Man, my dads Subaru, and an atlas. Now, in the big picture of the story, this particular song is one of the ones that outdates my commitment to the 18-21 timeframe. This song is just after the fact, but entirely necessary to build the foundation overall.

I was still dreaming of the woman I'd said good-bye to in Hawaii. She was a good woman, the kind of woman you try to hold on to. But, she was good at being free. And she taught me how to feel that way. I called her Creation's Daughter. She was fire, earth, wind, water. When I left the island, I didn't know when I would be coming back. It was a sacrifice I doubted at times when I felt alone and uncertain of the way, which was often in those days.

So, there I was, high as a kite, sitting on those big granite rocks in the middle of the Truckee River considering the journey I had just been on. I'd met my mother, spent a week with her, then headed south to meet up with two girl friends of mine. We'd driven to Burning Man together, only for me to then spend it alone with Sleepy as my friends went to their respected camps. I wasn't Nahko back then. I knew no one except Sleepy Brian and our trusty vehicles. Our steeds, our home. Funny how a big chunk of metal can become your closest friend.

Dust filled every pore, every orifice. It permeated the surface of my body and all I owned. There was a strange loneliness that would fill me up as I wandered through the crowded desert. Aliens, all of 'em. I would wake up in the morning and ride my bike over to a cafe I'd found that served chai. There was an old piano under their tent that beckoned me, and it became my routine to sip cold chai and hide from the sun playing on those ivories. There was a dead, dried out carcass of a cat laid atop that piano. And it seemed like every time I sat down on that bench someone would give me some LSD. I don't recall the songs that came out of me at that time, but I reckon the title of this

story is one of them. There is always an origin story to a song. Where the muse pushes, and the writer jots. For us crazy ones, it's hard to keep track of all of them, what with the tracers, fractal visions, and sound waves that chart each course.

The moment the sun went beyond the hill, I was sure that the playa became a landing pad and a beacon for all beings unseen. There was no way we could all be

"I was old enough to know better, I was young enough to keep trying."

there for any other reason. We were moon walkers, explorers and we were asking for a sign.

I slept under my car, wrapped in a tarp. When the water truck would pass by in the morning to settle the dust, I would run out beneath its falls and wash in its brown messy sparkles.

When we finally made it out of there, we went straight to the river; It would take days for the layers of dust to peel off our skin. Brian and I parted ways; he had a trim job waiting. So did I, but I had my dear lady friends to catch up with first. I did find them after a few days. My Subaru would be the aircraft through Reno, Lassen, the portals of Shasta, Weaverville, and onward to the Mendicino County Line. We found work together, and I began my new work as a digger of gold in the wild west. Those weeks spent with two jungle mountain sisters shifted my perspective on many things. The teachings of Kerouac were the teachings of a lonely man, disillusioned by the world, who found solace in alcohol, tarmac, and poetry. Sleepy in turn offered the ropes to psychedelics, indie rock, and fending for oneself alone on the road. These were important lessons and skills. It was only a matter of time before the ways of the witchy women reached me. These two brought me a gentleness and a sisterhood I had been missing. It was a rounding out that was needed. Those two listened to my songs and gave my self-esteem the biggest boost I didn't know it needed. I'd found my audience. I'd found my home. They taught me astrology, how to roll joints, to live with little, but eat healthily. To soften my blows, to think with compassion before acting with aggression, to give more and expect nothing in return. They reminded me of the power in Aloha. Truly. In a time where I could have wandered aimlessly and ended up anywhere, I was captured by two daughters of Creation and lifted into a new chapter.

There's a sense of longing drifting between bars here. A feeling of loss, yet not without a hint of redemption. To me, all the best road/love stories are filled with these sentiments. Walking through those old grandfather trees in Jedediah, I knew it was unlikely that my lover would return. Certainly, never in the same way. 'None of this will bring you back. As a wanderer, I must expect that.' Once again, the consequences of that endless highway and my commitment to it provided great lessons, but not so much the lover. I was old enough to know better. I was young enough to keep trying.

— 18 —

CREATION'S DAUGHTER

Stoned on a stone on the Truckee River.
So lost in thought oh the things I remember.

One of them's your pretty face. Another's
the things it would say. Things like:

All of these pivotal, obvious prophets.
They are the change and the change in your
pocket.

Always pushing for the moment. That you lose
control, but you just flow with it.

I have seen faces gathering in the desert.
Not to find god or to find an answer.

Just to be a part of the possibilities of
thousands of bodies creating energy.

Well, out here there's certainly alien activ-
ity. But, where is here? Are we separate
from reality?

Maybe we've landed on the moon! Hope I don't
have to leave anytime soon.

I worked those hills in the wild, wild west.
And there I found gold and knowledge and respect.

But, none of this will bring you back. As a
wanderer I must expect that.

Followed a rooster to the mouth of a portal.
I am an ox and I'm tired of these mortals.

Cleansing in the coastal waters. I fell in
love with the daughter of creation.

And how I lost her's another story to tell.

— 19 —

SUSANNA
I'm Only Passing Through

In my book, this is the quintessential rendition. Here is the classic tale of the lonely traveller; reminded of the muse acting as the compass, pointing in all directions, bound in unconditional love. She is limitless in her freedom, but not without boundaries.

I can't remember when I started rewriting this classic folk traditional. Somewhere in the back of my brain, there's a memory of sitting in our little shanty in Hamakua watching the rain fall and humming it. Sometimes that's how songs start. Watching nature, drifting into memories of loss or love or loss of love and then my hands start strumming. Before you know it, there's an idea being birthed.

For some of us, the road becomes our lover. She is always with you, never questions, but provides plenty of struggle and chaos to overcome. When one drifts, especially as much as I did at that age, you begin to wonder if you'll always be the wind. You wonder if you'll land and become attached, only to get caught in another swell and float away. It becomes a task to live unattached, but attached to being unattached. It's an adventure to live in the unknown like that each day, with only your memories of the muse that you left behind. To sleep under the stars and wonder if you'll ever find it again. It's a strange thing, belonging to the desolate. An odd kinship to the vagabond, barely surviving parts of creation. I remember wanting to know what it was like to live unseen amongst the rats, yet knowing I didn't have a choice either. The matrix was so complex, and I was yet to discover the tools to play the game and stay under the radar. But, love, or our search for it, is a powerful ally and a sword worth wielding when you've got nothing to lose and everything to discover.

At a juncture I would soon come to know all too well, I had to make a choice: the road or the woman. More often than not, I chose the road. My lover became my moment. My moment became my way. Until, well... that's another story for another time.

— 20 —

SUSANNA

I left my home for the open road bid farewell
to a beautiful girl

She was out to push and prod my bravery
I was out to conquer the world.

While I was circling the globe she'd spin
hers point somewhere and then

She'd say I fell in love with a drifters son
and now he's gone again.

I held my adventures up like trophies high
over my head

Susanna she's a patience woman she praised my
happiness.

I'd sing oh Susanna don't you cry for me

I'm headed for those coastal waters an ocean
for to see.

I saw your face carved in the caves in the
tunneling fields

I wore my stubbornness like armor a reliable
shield

Oh how could I have been so thoughtless and
careless with my love

When I met you you were drifting too just
like the driftwood does

SUSANNA

She'd be knee deep in the waters whispering
to the sea

Susanna she's a graceful woman her words have
convinced me

I'd sing oh Susanna why don't you come down
here with me

We'll play in the oldest parts of the jungle
and climb a banyan tree.

Explore from shore to shore there's always
one more mountain to see

Susanna came to me in a dream and on the
summit she said to me

She said I am freedom I'm all that you seek

But you can't have this if you want all that
and you certainly can't have me.

Oh Susanna I don't cry for you

You're the best adventure I've had yet
but I'm only passing through.

— 21 —

HAMAKUA
The Breath of God

This song is a little rogue diamond. I snuck it in. I didn't write it during the same young days as all of the others. But I just couldn't not put this song on the record. It is such a crucial tune that defines this time, even though it was a little later in the timeline. I was probably nearly 22 when I wrote this song. I had already come back to Hawaii after meeting my mom, traveling Northern California, going to Burning Man, and now was living on the 'farm' with 'ol 7 Feathers (Jason Fox). I had spent a few months on Kona side after returning to the aina picking coffee and sleeping in my truck. Jason called me and invited me to come live with him. It made sense. I'd already helped him with a few building projects the year before, and now more than ever it seemed we both were in search of brotherhood. There was a deeper vision was to be explored. It would be there, in the rolling hills of Hamakua where many of the songs of Medicine for the People would be born. I'll never forget those first three years living in the mist of what the Kanaka Maoli called Creator's Breath.

Those were some hard years too. Jason brought me in and allowed me to claim my stake there in that soil. We became a team. He showed me the ropes of hammer and nail, and I earned my place. We both worked a number of jobs to stay afloat. Construction, landscaping, picking fruit, tree trimming, and whatever else could stack a few bills. Most the money we made would get reinvested in daily living expenses, farm tools, or trees and plants. On days off, we would explore the jungles and waterfalls that surrounded and bordered the 23-acre parcel. Truly, this was a playground paradise, and we got to know every nook and cranny.

There was a particular tree down by the waterfall where we would shower that was a favourite of mine. It was the only Ohia on the property, and it cast its long branches over that water as if it was its guardian. Ohia takes a long time to grow. In fact, it is the first tree to grow from the lava, so when you see one you know it has been there for a long time. I figured if that tree could have the patience to grow through the darkness and into the light, well, so could I. That perch would be my place of refuge when Jason and I had our differences. You see, I'm an Aquarian. Jason, he's a Taurean. Both of us fiercely independent. It's safe to say we butted heads from time to time. Years later, I realized how impatient I was with him. I wanted to evolve more rapidly, to be air, try things out, let it flow. Jason liked his ways, fiercely earth, and was much slower to change. Needless to say, in my youth, I was a firecracker. Perhaps some would say I still am.

   In the last verse, I touch on some youthful phi-losophy I'd decided on about relationships and love. Instead of focusing on pining after someone I wanted to keep and be just for me, my medicine became the fact that people always leave. Lovers come and go. With that in mind at that time, I could try to live without the suffering from the departure of the physical, to be present in each moment, and live in gratitude for time well spent. Each notch I climbed in my great wall to consciousness led me higher to reasoning. I let my first archetype die, little by little. After all, be-fore Hamakua who the hell was I?

"While the earth still moves, do all you can."

— 22 —

HAMAKUA

Before Hamakua, who the hell were ya?
And do you know by now?

Remember the waiting for water falling?
Concentrating on myself.

The quiet ohia gave me the fever.
To push thru cracks and reach for light.

Oi Kau Kala E Hana I Ola Honua

Before 7 feathers gave me his sweater.
I'd be the brave and bare the cold.

I found myself seeking a false understanding
of what is truth and honesty.

I kept on stretching out all of his blessings
and learned to scream above the rain.

Oi Kau Kala E Hana I Ola Honua

Before my beloved took me for granted.
I would face the lion's den.

Through our indecision I discovered
my medicine.

People staying, people leaving.

HAMAKUA

For what a better lesson than to be
open to the messages.

Coming through in spurts and mumbles!

Oi Kau Kala E Hana I Ola Honua

— 23 —

DIE LIKE DINOZ
Centered in the Center

There once lived two dinosaurs. They were young and in love with each other and the idyllic land which they called home. Everything was a dream; there wasn't a time more fruitful and vibrant. Suddenly one day, it all changed. Mother earth farted, basically, and the climate changed. Ice caps melted, fires swallowed forests, and great storms flooded the plains. With these huge planetary shifts, two ancient lovers were torn apart. Only heartbreak endured for them in that interim. The Great Mother spent decades reforming and seeding the soil. Both dinosaurs thought that surely the other was long dead. Acceptance was difficult. For where is home if not with your love?

And then one day, it happened again. Plates shifted, valleys swelled, and mountains moved. A land bridge formed. Many, in fact. Years still passed before they walked on the edges of the same forest. Something was different that day, and each knew it as a corner was rounded, and a glimpse was finally caught of each other. It had been lifetimes. How do dinosaurs hug? I'm not sure, but I'll bet you it's prehistoric. Not one has been recorded. A shame. I reckon the world could stand to learn a thing or two about dino hugs. Anyways, back to the reunion. Hearts warmed with a re-newed sense of purpose. A time away that recalibrated them both to face the challenges of the future, but certainly left no damage done to the loyalty of their heart's song. And now, to begin again. The dance. To kindle the fire. To kneel at our Great Mother's power and mercy.

But, I don't always tell the story like that.

I used to live in a treehouse. Part-time, of course, the other half spent up the Hamakua coast. My cosmic

copy had built it, and that's where I remember sitting in the corner doorway looking out at the lava rock and guava trees, tripping on these moon booms, free styling the infinite chasms of my channel. My lover, I called my cosmic copy. She was my greatest teacher at that time. One who ushered me quite properly into my early 20's and defined the kind of man I would soon become. She emboldened my lust for action and thrust me with loving kindness in front of my fears. Whatever reluctance I'd been carrying was promptly forgotten, and I learned to play hard and fall like a ninja. Everything was in slow motion back then. Information came in strong waves, like bamboo swaying or the Iou circling above our heads as we road bareback towards the mountain. A lifestyle was forming. Barefoot and shirtless. Fingernails spotted with dirt and skin speckled with jungle and oceanic scars. Free of artificial flavors and filled with farm fresh foods. Guarded, but openly concerned for the fate of humanity in a collapsing world habitat. At times it seemed terrifying to know what I knew of peace and tranquility living such a DIY life on a small island deep in the piko of the Pacific. Maybe I knew it wouldn't last forever, that one day I would have to leave my oasis and cultivate my garden around the world. There is a bottomless feeling of mortality in this song. Yet, as hollow as it feels in moments, it is clearly laced with gratitude for the breath of life and for the soil to which we eventually will return. It's as if I was saying, 'I am with you, beloved. Over mountains, across oceans. Let us sing praises to the most high. For what else is there to do, but to live vertically, with a well-kept flame, and sing into the emptiness with joy and fever.' After all, we all must find our own way home.

"We All Must Find Our Own Way Home."

— 24 —

DIE LIKE DINOZ

I will die from rising tides.
From never ending winters

No potable water. No real food left.
Just artificial flavors

But oh my love what's left is centered
to center

But in the middle I'll sing your name
out loud

And it will sound like this coming from
my lips above the trees it reaches

And it will be a sound that dissipates
but penetrates all of your senses

You'll hear something like this something
like this, once in a while yeah once in a
while

And you will go, go very far.
And you will do the work at hand

And when you are done. You will go home.
Right where you've been all along.

Well, over all those mountain ranges.
Across all bodies of water

I keep drifting back into providing arms of
daughters

No more waiting. No more telling.
She says I doubt man will see

But I mean I hope he does though I know he
won't because

That's just not how it's meant to be.
But I'd like to stay with you for a while

Though I know our hours are dwindling

And if that fire goes unattended, I will
gather kindling

I'll sing these songs

I'll sing the praises and glories

I'll sing these songs into the gray
overcast mornings

I will live in story shaping lover curving
in each likeness

She words it nicely cosmic copy baring weight
and bearing fruit

We're finding opposition in recycled opinions
floating stagnant and very horizontal

And it's clear to me it's quite a vertical
thing we all must find our own way home

But to live life like this it takes must
practice breaking habits born into

And oh my love we were created carnivores and
much like dinosaurs we will die

But live forever yes forever in the soil from
which we came

DIE LIKE DINOZ

And we'll sing these songs

We'll sing the praises and glories

We'll sing these songs into the gray
overcast mornings

There will come a great change and when it
comes there won't be room for everyone

To go see what's left to see

What's left to see?

Merely shapes and land mass shifting

What's left to see?

Merely shapes and land mass shifting

— the beginning —

#MYNAMEISBEAR

#MEDICINETRIBE